Contents

Preface to the 450th Anniversary Edition 5

Introduction 7

The Heidelberg Catechism

Comfort (Q&A 1-2) 8

Part I: Misery (Q&A 3-11) 9

Part II: Deliverance (Q&A 12-85) 12
God the Father (Q&A 26-28) 18
God the Son (Q&A 29-52) 20
God the Holy Spirit (Q&A 53-64) 31
The Holy Sacraments (Q&A 65-85) 38
Holy Baptism (Q&A 69-74) 40
The Holy Supper of Jesus Christ (Q&A 75-85) 43

Part III: Gratitude (Q&A 86-129) 51
The Ten Commandments (Q&A 92-115) 53
The Lord's Prayer (Q&A 116-129) 67

Preface
to the 450th Anniversary Edition

Perhaps the most well-known and widely used of the Reformation catechisms, the Heidelberg Catechism has been admired for its clarity as an expression of the Reformed Christian faith as well as for its warm and personal tone. Many of its questions and answers—especially Q&A 1—have been memorized by thousands and have become an anchor for faith. In 2013 we celebrate the 450th anniversary of this classic and beloved catechism.

This 450th Anniversary Edition of the Heidelberg Catechism is a fresh and accurate translation (completed in 2011) from the 1563 German and Latin texts, using the 1988 translation by the Christian Reformed Church in North America as an English-language base. This edition is also an ecumenical effort in that it is now the officially recognized translation for use in the Christian Reformed Church in North America, the Presbyterian Church (USA), and the Reformed Church in America (RCA). This development fits the Heidelberg Catechism's original purpose, which was not only to teach the faith but also to unite various church factions in the sixteenth-century German Palatinate by means of a common confession.

We thank the following for their important and faithful work on the joint translation committee:

- Lyle Bierma (CRC, Calvin Theological Seminary)
- J. Todd Billings (RCA, Western Theological Seminary)
- Eugene Heideman (RCA, Western Theological Seminary, emeritus)
- Charles White (RCA staff)
- Leonard J. Vander Zee (CRC staff)
- Dawn Devries (Union Presbyterian Seminary)
- David Stubbs (Western Theological Seminary)

It is our prayer that this book will deepen the faith of our churches, further unite us in our common confessions, and serve as a testimony to the historic Reformed faith as a gift to the whole church.

—Leonard J. Vander Zee, Theological Editor,
Faith Alive Christian Resources

The Heidelberg Catechism

Introduction

The Heidelberg Catechism (1563) was composed in the city of Heidelberg, Germany, at the request of Elector Frederick III, who ruled the province of the Palatinate from 1559 to 1576. The new catechism was intended as a tool for teaching young people, a guide for preaching in the provincial churches, and a form of confessional unity among the several Protestant factions in the Palatinate. An old tradition credits Zacharias Ursinus and Caspar Olevianus with being the coauthors of the catechism, but the project was actually the work of a team of ministers and university theologians under the watchful eye of Frederick himself. Ursinus probably served as the primary writer on the team, and Olevianus had a lesser role. The catechism was approved by a synod in Heidelberg in January 1563. A second and third German edition, each with small additions, as well as a Latin translation were published the same year in Heidelberg. The third edition was included in the Palatinate Church Order of November 15, 1563, at which time the catechism was divided into fifty-two sections or Lord's Days, so that one Lord's Day could be explained in an afternoon worship service each Sunday of the year.

The Synod of Dort approved the Heidelberg Catechism in 1619, and it soon became the most ecumenical of the Reformed catechisms and confessions. It has been translated into many European, Asian, and African languages and is still the most widely used and warmly praised catechism of the Reformation period.

Most of the footnoted biblical references in this translation of the catechism were included in the early German and Latin editions, but the precise selection was approved by Synod 1975 of the Christian Reformed Church.

1   Q. **What is your only comfort
in life and in death?**

       A. That I am not my own,[1]
but belong—
body and soul,
in life and in death—[2]
to my faithful Savior, Jesus Christ.[3]

He has fully paid for all my sins with his precious blood,[4]
and has set me free from the tyranny of the devil.[5]
He also watches over me in such a way[6]
that not a hair can fall from my head
without the will of my Father in heaven;[7]
in fact, all things must work together for my salvation.[8]

Because I belong to him,
Christ, by his Holy Spirit,
assures me of eternal life[9]
and makes me wholeheartedly willing and ready
from now on to live for him.[10]

[1] 1 Cor. 6:19-20
[2] Rom. 14:7-9
[3] 1 Cor. 3:23; Titus 2:14
[4] 1 Pet. 1:18-19; 1 John 1:7-9; 2:2
[5] John 8:34-36; Heb. 2:14-15; 1 John 3:1-11
[6] John 6:39-40; 10:27-30; 2 Thess. 3:3; 1 Pet. 1:5
[7] Matt. 10:29-31; Luke 21:16-18
[8] Rom. 8:28
[9] Rom. 8:15-16; 2 Cor. 1:21-22; 5:5; Eph. 1:13-14
[10] Rom. 8:1-17

2   Q. **What must you know to
live and die in the joy of this comfort?**

       A. Three things:
first, how great my sin and misery are;[1]
second, how I am set free from all my sins and misery;[2]
third, how I am to thank God for such deliverance.[3]

[1] Rom. 3:9-10; 1 John 1:10
[2] John 17:3; Acts 4:12; 10:43
[3] Matt. 5:16; Rom. 6:13; Eph. 5:8-10; 2 Tim. 2:15; 1 Pet. 2:9-10

Part I: Misery

LORD'S DAY 2

3   Q. How do you come to know your misery?
**   A.** The law of God tells me.[1]

[1] Rom. 3:20; 7:7-25

4   Q. What does God's law require of us?
**   A.** Christ teaches us this in summary in Matthew 22:37-40:

> "'You shall love the Lord your God
> with all your heart,
> and with all your soul,
> and with all your mind.'[1]
> This is the greatest and first commandment.

> "And a second is like it:
> 'You shall love your neighbor as yourself.'[2]

> "On these two commandments hang
> all the law and the prophets."

[1] Deut. 6:5
[2] Lev. 19:18

5   Q. Can you live up to all this perfectly?
**   A.** No.[1]
     I have a natural tendency
     to hate God and my neighbor.[2]

[1] Rom. 3:9-20, 23; 1 John 1:8, 10
[2] Gen. 6:5; Jer. 17:9; Rom. 7:23-24; 8:7; Eph. 2:1-3; Titus 3:3

6   Q. **Did God create people
        so wicked and perverse?**
     A. No.
        God created them good[1] and in his own image,[2]
            that is, in true righteousness and holiness,[3]
        so that they might
            truly know God their creator,[4]
            love him with all their heart,
            and live with God in eternal happiness,
        to praise and glorify him.[5]

[1] Gen. 1:31
[2] Gen. 1:26-27
[3] Eph. 4:24
[4] Col. 3:10
[5] Ps. 8

7   Q. **Then where does this corrupt human nature come from?**
     A. The fall and disobedience of our first parents,
            Adam and Eve, in Paradise.[1]
        This fall has so poisoned our nature[2]
            that we are all conceived and born
            in a sinful condition.[3]

[1] Gen. 3
[2] Rom. 5:12, 18-19
[3] Ps. 51:5

8   Q. **But are we so corrupt
        that we are totally unable to do any good
        and inclined toward all evil?**
     A. Yes,[1] unless we are born again
        by the Spirit of God.[2]

[1] Gen. 6:5; 8:21; Job 14:4; Isa. 53:6
[2] John 3:3-5

9   Q.   **But doesn't God do us an injustice**
             by requiring in his law
             what we are unable to do?

      A.   No, God created human beings with the ability to keep the law.[1]
          They, however, provoked by the devil,[2]
             in willful disobedience,[3]
             robbed themselves and all their descendants of these gifts.[4]

[1] Gen. 1:31; Eph. 4:24
[2] Gen. 3:13; John 8:44
[3] Gen. 3:6
[4] Rom. 5:12, 18, 19

10   Q.   **Does God permit**
             such disobedience and rebellion
             to go unpunished?

      A.   Certainly not.
          God is terribly angry
             with the sin we are born with
             as well as the sins we personally commit.

          As a just judge,
          God will punish them both now and in eternity,[1]
          having declared:
             "Cursed is everyone who does not observe and obey
             all the things written in the book of the law."[2]

[1] Ex. 34:7; Ps. 5:4-6; Nah. 1:2; Rom. 1:18; Eph. 5:6; Heb. 9:27
[2] Gal. 3:10; Deut. 27:26

11   Q.   **But isn't God also merciful?**

      A.   God is certainly merciful,[1]
          but also just.[2]
          God's justice demands
             that sin, committed against his supreme majesty,
             be punished with the supreme penalty—
             eternal punishment of body and soul.[3]

[1] Ex. 34:6-7; Ps. 103:8-9
[2] Ex. 34:7; Deut. 7:9-11; Ps. 5:4-6; Heb. 10:30-31
[3] Matt. 25:35-46

LORD'S DAY 5

12 Q. **According to God's righteous judgment**
      we deserve punishment
      both now and in eternity:
      how then can we escape this punishment
      and return to God's favor?
   A. God requires that his justice be satisfied.[1]
      Therefore the claims of this justice
      must be paid in full,
      either by ourselves or by another.[2]

[1] Ex. 23:7; Rom. 2:1-11
[2] Isa. 53:11; Rom. 8:3-4

13 Q. **Can we make this payment ourselves?**
   A. Certainly not.
      Actually, we increase our debt every day.[1]

[1] Matt. 6:12; Rom. 2:4-5

14 Q. **Can another creature—any at all—**
      pay this debt for us?
   A. No.
      To begin with,
          God will not punish any other creature
          for what a human is guilty of.[1]
      Furthermore,
          no mere creature can bear the weight
          of God's eternal wrath against sin
          and deliver others from it.[2]

[1] Ezek. 18:4, 20; Heb. 2:14-18
[2] Ps. 49:7-9; 130:3

15 Q. **What kind of mediator and deliverer**
      should we look for then?
   A. One who is a true[1] and righteous[2] human,
          yet more powerful than all creatures,
          that is, one who is also true God.[3]

[1] Rom. 1:3; 1 Cor. 15:21; Heb. 2:17
[2] Isa. 53:9; 2 Cor. 5:21; Heb. 7:26
[3] Isa. 7:14; 9:6; Jer. 23:6; John 1:1

16 Q. Why must the mediator be a true and righteous human?
    A. God's justice demands
        that human nature, which has sinned,
        must pay for sin;[1]
        but a sinful human could never pay for others.[2]

[1] Rom. 5:12, 15; 1 Cor. 15:21; Heb. 2:14-16
[2] Heb. 7:26-27; 1 Pet. 3:18

17 Q. Why must the mediator also be true God?
    A. So that the mediator,
        by the power of his divinity,
        might bear the weight of God's wrath in his humanity
        and earn for us
        and restore to us
        righteousness and life.[1]

[1] Isa. 53; John 3:16; 2 Cor. 5:21

18 Q. Then who is this mediator—
       true God and at the same time
       a true and righteous human?
    A. Our Lord Jesus Christ,[1]
        who was given to us
        to completely deliver us
        and make us right with God.[2]

[1] Matt. 1:21-23; Luke 2:11; 1 Tim. 2:5
[2] 1 Cor. 1:30

19 Q. How do you come to know this?

A. The holy gospel tells me.

God began to reveal the gospel already in Paradise;[1]
later God proclaimed it
  by the holy patriarchs[2] and prophets[3]
and foreshadowed it
  by the sacrifices and other ceremonies of the law;[4]
and finally God fulfilled it
  through his own beloved Son.[5]

[1] Gen. 3:15
[2] Gen. 22:18; 49:10
[3] Isa. 53; Jer. 23:5-6; Mic. 7:18-20; Acts 10:43; Heb. 1:1-2
[4] Lev. 1-7; John 5:46; Heb. 10:1-10
[5] Rom. 10:4; Gal. 4:4-5; Col. 2:17

20 **Q.** **Are all people then saved through Christ just as they were lost through Adam?**
     A. No.
         Only those are saved
         who through true faith
             are grafted into Christ
             and accept all his benefits.[1]

[1] Matt. 7:14; John 3:16, 18, 36; Rom. 11:16-21

21 **Q.** **What is true faith?**
     A. True faith is
         not only a sure knowledge by which I hold as true
             all that God has revealed to us in Scripture;[1]
         it is also a wholehearted trust,[2]
             which the Holy Spirit creates in me[3] by the gospel,[4]
             that God has freely granted,
                 not only to others but to me also,[5]
                 forgiveness of sins,
                 eternal righteousness,
                 and salvation.[6]
         These are gifts of sheer grace,
             granted solely by Christ's merit.[7]

[1] John 17:3, 17; Heb. 11:1-3; James 2:19
[2] Rom. 4:18-21; 5:1; 10:10; Heb. 4:14-16
[3] Matt. 16:15-17; John 3:5; Acts 16:14
[4] Rom. 1:16; 10:17; 1 Cor. 1:21
[5] Gal. 2:20
[6] Rom. 1:17; Heb. 10:10
[7] Rom. 3:21-26; Gal. 2:16; Eph. 2:8-10

22 Q. What then must a Christian believe?

A. All that is promised us in the gospel,[1]
     a summary of which is taught us
     in the articles of our universal
     and undisputed Christian faith.

[1] Matt. 28:18-20; John 20:30-31

23 Q. What are these articles?

A. I believe in God, the Father almighty,
     creator of heaven and earth.

I believe in Jesus Christ, his only begotten Son, our Lord,
     who was conceived by the Holy Spirit
     and born of the virgin Mary.
     He suffered under Pontius Pilate,
     was crucified, died, and was buried;
     he descended to hell.
     The third day he rose again from the dead.
     He ascended to heaven
     and is seated at the right hand of God the Father almighty.
     From there he will come to judge the living and the dead.

I believe in the Holy Spirit,
     the holy catholic church,
     the communion of saints,
     the forgiveness of sins,
     the resurrection of the body,
     and the life everlasting. Amen.

24 Q. How are these articles divided?
  A. Into three parts:
      God the Father and our creation;
      God the Son and our deliverance;
      and God the Holy Spirit and our sanctification.

**25 Q. Since there is only one divine being,[1]
      why do you speak of three:
      Father, Son, and Holy Spirit?**
  A. Because that is how
      God has revealed himself in his Word:[2]
      these three distinct persons
      are one, true, eternal God.

[1] Deut. 6:4; 1 Cor. 8:4, 6
[2] Matt. 3:16-17; 28:18-19; Luke 4:18 (Isa. 61:1); John 14:26; 15:26; 2 Cor. 13:14; Gal. 4:6;
  Tit. 3:5-6

LORD'S DAY 9

26 Q. **What do you believe when you say,
"I believe in God, the Father almighty,
creator of heaven and earth"?**
   A. That the eternal Father of our Lord Jesus Christ,
      who out of nothing created heaven and earth
         and everything in them,[1]
      who still upholds and rules them
         by his eternal counsel and providence,[2]
   is my God and Father
      because of Christ the Son.[3]

   I trust God so much that I do not doubt
      he will provide
         whatever I need
         for body and soul,[4]
      and will turn to my good
         whatever adversity he sends upon me
         in this sad world.[5]

   God is able to do this because he is almighty God[6]
   and desires to do this because he is a faithful Father.[7]

[1] Gen. 1-2; Ex. 20:11; Ps. 33:6; Isa. 44:24; Acts 4:24; 14:15
[2] Ps. 104; Matt. 6:30; 10:29; Eph. 1:11
[3] John 1:12-13; Rom. 8:15-16; Gal. 4:4-7; Eph. 1:5
[4] Ps. 55:22; Matt. 6:25-26; Luke 12:22-31
[5] Rom. 8:28
[6] Gen. 18:14; Rom. 8:31-39
[7] Matt. 7:9-11

27 Q. **What do you understand**
    by the providence of God?
    A. The almighty and ever present power of God[1]
        by which God upholds, as with his hand,
            heaven
            and earth
            and all creatures,[2]
        and so rules them that
            leaf and blade,
            rain and drought,
            fruitful and lean years,
            food and drink,
            health and sickness,
            prosperity and poverty—[3]
        all things, in fact,
        come to us
            not by chance[4]
            but by his fatherly hand.[5]

[1] Jer. 23:23-24; Acts 17:24-28
[2] Heb. 1:3
[3] Jer. 5:24; Acts 14:15-17; John 9:3; Prov. 22:2
[4] Prov. 16:33
[5] Matt. 10:29

28 Q. **How does the knowledge**
    of God's creation and providence help us?
    A. We can be patient when things go against us,[1]
        thankful when things go well,[2]
        and for the future we can have
        good confidence in our faithful God and Father
        that nothing in creation will separate us from his love.[3]
        For all creatures are so completely in God's hand
            that without his will
            they can neither move nor be moved.[4]

[1] Job 1:21-22; James 1:3
[2] Deut. 8:10; 1 Thess. 5:18
[3] Ps. 55:22; Rom. 5:3-5; 8:38-39
[4] Job 1:12; 2:6; Prov. 21:1; Acts 17:24-28

LORD'S DAY 11

29 Q. **Why is the Son of God called "Jesus,"**
       meaning "savior"?
   A. Because he saves us from our sins,[1]
       and because salvation should not be sought
       and cannot be found in anyone else.[2]

[1] Matt. 1:21; Heb. 7:25
[2] Isa. 43:11; John 15:5; Acts 4:11-12; 1 Tim. 2:5

30 Q. **Do those who look for**
       their salvation in saints,
       in themselves, or elsewhere
       really believe in the only savior Jesus?
   A. No.
       Although they boast of being his,
       by their actions they deny
       the only savior, Jesus.[1]

       Either Jesus is not a perfect savior,
       or those who in true faith accept this savior
       have in him all they need for their salvation.[2]

[1] 1 Cor. 1:12-13; Gal. 5:4
[2] Col. 1:19-20; 2:10; 1 John 1:7

31 **Q. Why is he called "Christ,"
meaning "anointed"?**

A. Because he has been ordained by God the Father
and has been anointed with the Holy Spirit[1]
to be
our chief prophet and teacher[2]
who fully reveals to us
the secret counsel and will of God concerning our
deliverance;[3]
our only high priest[4]
who has delivered us by the one sacrifice of his body,[5]
and who continually pleads our cause with the Father;[6]
and our eternal king[7]
who governs us by his Word and Spirit,
and who guards us and keeps us
in the freedom he has won for us.[8]

[1] Luke 3:21-22; 4:14-19 (Isa. 61:1); Heb. 1:9 (Ps. 45:7)
[2] Acts 3:22 (Deut. 18:15)
[3] John 1:18; 15:15
[4] Heb. 7:17 (Ps. 110:4)
[5] Heb. 9:12; 10:11-14
[6] Rom. 8:34; Heb. 9:24
[7] Matt. 21:5 (Zech. 9:9)
[8] Matt. 28:18-20; John 10:28; Rev. 12:10-11

32 **Q. But why are you called a Christian?**

A. Because by faith I am a member of Christ[1]
and so I share in his anointing.[2]
I am anointed
to confess his name,[3]
to present myself to him as a living sacrifice of thanks,[4]
to strive with a free conscience against sin and the devil
in this life,[5]
and afterward to reign with Christ
over all creation
for eternity.[6]

[1] 1 Cor. 12:12-27
[2] Acts 2:17 (Joel 2:28); 1 John 2:27
[3] Matt. 10:32; Rom. 10:9-10; Heb. 13:15
[4] Rom. 12:1; 1 Pet. 2:5, 9
[5] Gal. 5:16-17; Eph. 6:11; 1 Tim. 1:18-19
[6] Matt. 25:34; 2 Tim. 2:12

**33 Q. Why is he called God's "only begotten Son"
when we also are God's children?**
    A. Because Christ alone is the eternal, natural Son of God.[1]
        We, however, are adopted children of God—
           adopted by grace through Christ.[2]

[1] John 1:1-3, 14, 18; Heb. 1
[2] John 1:12; Rom. 8:14-17; Eph. 1:5-6

34 Q. Why do you call him "our Lord"?
    A. Because—
        not with gold or silver,
           but with his precious blood—[1]
        he has set us free
           from sin and from the tyranny of the devil,[2]
        and has bought us,
           body and soul,
        to be his very own.[3]

[1] 1 Pet. 1:18-19
[2] Col. 1:13-14; Heb. 2:14-15
[3] 1 Cor. 6:20; 1 Tim. 2:5-6

35 Q. **What does it mean that he**
        "was conceived by the Holy Spirit
        and born of the virgin Mary"?
    A. That the eternal Son of God,
            who is and remains
            true and eternal God,[1]
        took to himself,
            through the working of the Holy Spirit,[2]
            from the flesh and blood of the virgin Mary,[3]
        a truly human nature
            so that he might also become David's true descendant,[4]
            like his brothers and sisters in every way[5]
                except for sin.[6]

[1] John 1:1; 10:30-36; Acts 13:33 (Ps. 2:7); Col. 1:15-17; 1 John 5:20
[2] Luke 1:35
[3] Matt. 1:18-23; John 1:14; Gal. 4:4; Heb. 2:14
[4] 2 Sam. 7:12-16; Ps. 132:11; Matt. 1:1; Rom. 1:3
[5] Phil. 2:7; Heb. 2:17
[6] Heb. 4:15; 7:26-27

36 Q. **How does the holy conception and birth of Christ**
        benefit you?
    A. He is our mediator[1]
        and, in God's sight,
        he covers with his innocence and perfect holiness
        my sinfulness in which I was conceived.[2]

[1] 1 Tim. 2:5-6; Heb. 9:13-15
[2] Rom. 8:3-4; 2 Cor. 5:21; Gal. 4:4-5; 1 Pet. 1:18-19

37 Q. **What do you understand
        by the word "suffered"?**
    A. That during his whole life on earth,
        but especially at the end,
        Christ sustained
            in body and soul
            the wrath of God against the sin of the whole human race.[1]

    This he did in order that,
        by his suffering as the only atoning sacrifice,[2]
        he might deliver us, body and soul,
            from eternal condemnation,[3]
        and gain for us
            God's grace,
            righteousness,
            and eternal life.[4]

[1] Isa. 53; 1 Pet. 2:24; 3:18
[2] Rom. 3:25; Heb. 10:14; 1 John 2:2; 4:10
[3] Rom. 8:1-4; Gal. 3:13
[4] John 3:16; Rom. 3:24-26

38 Q. **Why did he suffer
        "under Pontius Pilate" as judge?**
    A. So that he,
            though innocent,
        might be condemned by an earthly judge,[1]
        and so free us from the severe judgment of God
            that was to fall on us.[2]

[1] Luke 23:13-24; John 19:4, 12-16
[2] Isa. 53:4-5; 2 Cor. 5:21; Gal. 3:13

39 Q. **Is it significant that he was "crucified"
        instead of dying some other way?**
    A. Yes.
        By this I am convinced
        that he shouldered the curse
        which lay on me,
        since death by crucifixion was cursed by God.[1]

[1] Gal. 3:10-13 (Deut. 21:23)

40 Q. Why did Christ have to suffer death?
    A. Because God's justice and truth require it: [1]
        nothing else could pay for our sins
        except the death of the Son of God. [2]

[1] Gen. 2:17
[2] Rom. 8:3-4; Phil. 2:8; Heb. 2:9

41 Q. Why was he "buried"?
    A. His burial testifies
        that he really died. [1]

[1] Isa. 53:9; John 19:38-42; Acts 13:29; 1 Cor. 15:3-4

42 Q. Since Christ has died for us,
      why do we still have to die?
    A. Our death does not pay the debt of our sins. [1]
        Rather, it puts an end to our sinning
        and is our entrance into eternal life. [2]

[1] Ps. 49:7
[2] John 5:24; Phil. 1:21-23; 1 Thess. 5:9-10

43 Q. What further benefit do we receive
      from Christ's sacrifice and death on the cross?
    A. By Christ's power
        our old selves are crucified, put to death, and buried with him, [1]
        so that the evil desires of the flesh
           may no longer rule us, [2]
        but that instead we may offer ourselves
           as a sacrifice of gratitude to him. [3]

[1] Rom. 6:5-11; Col. 2:11-12
[2] Rom. 6:12-14
[3] Rom. 12:1; Eph. 5:1-2

**44 Q. Why does the creed add,
"He descended to hell"?**

   A. To assure me during attacks of deepest dread and temptation
   that Christ my Lord,
   > by suffering unspeakable anguish, pain, and terror of soul,
   >> on the cross but also earlier,
   > has delivered me from hellish anguish and torment.[1]

[1] Isa. 53; Matt. 26:36-46; 27:45-46; Luke 22:44; Heb. 5:7-10

**45 Q. How does Christ's resurrection
      benefit us?**

   A. First, by his resurrection he has overcome death,
      so that he might make us share in the righteousness
      he obtained for us by his death.[1]

   Second, by his power we too
      are already raised to a new life.[2]

   Third, Christ's resurrection
      is a sure pledge to us of our blessed resurrection.[3]

[1] Rom. 4:25; 1 Cor. 15:16-20; 1 Pet. 1:3-5
[2] Rom. 6:5-11; Eph. 2:4-6; Col. 3:1-4
[3] Rom. 8:11; 1 Cor. 15:12-23; Phil. 3:20-21

**46 Q. What do you mean by saying,
"He ascended to heaven"?**

 A. That Christ,
     while his disciples watched,
     was taken up from the earth into heaven[1]
     and remains there on our behalf[2]
     until he comes again
       to judge the living and the dead.[3]

[1] Luke 24:50-51; Acts 1:9-11
[2] Rom. 8:34; Eph. 4:8-10; Heb. 7:23-25; 9:24
[3] Acts 1:11

**47 Q. But isn't Christ with us
until the end of the world
as he promised us?[1]**

 A. Christ is true human and true God.
     In his human nature Christ is not now on earth;[2]
     but in his divinity, majesty, grace, and Spirit
     he is never absent from us.[3]

[1] Matt. 28:20
[2] Acts 1:9-11; 3:19-21
[3] Matt. 28:18-20; John 14:16-19

**48 Q. If his humanity is not present
wherever his divinity is,
then aren't the two natures of Christ
separated from each other?**

 A. Certainly not.
     Since divinity
       is not limited
       and is present everywhere,[1]
     it is evident that
       Christ's divinity is surely beyond the bounds of
         the humanity that has been taken on,
       but at the same time his divinity is in
       and remains personally united to
         his humanity.[2]

[1] Jer. 23:23-24; Acts 7:48-49 (Isa. 66:1)
[2] John 1:14; 3:13; Col. 2:9

**49 Q. How does Christ's ascension to heaven
   benefit us?**

   A. First, he is our advocate
         in heaven
         in the presence of his Father.[1]

      Second, we have our own flesh in heaven
         as a sure pledge that Christ our head
         will also take us, his members,
         up to himself.[2]

      Third, he sends his Spirit to us on earth
         as a corresponding pledge.[3]
         By the Spirit's power
            we seek not earthly things
            but the things above, where Christ is,
               sitting at God's right hand.[4]

[1] Rom. 8:34; 1 John 2:1
[2] John 14:2; 17:24; Eph. 2:4-6
[3] John 14:16; 2 Cor. 1:21-22; 5:5
[4] Col. 3:1-4

**50 Q. Why the next words:
"and is seated at the right hand of God"?**

A. Because Christ ascended to heaven
to show there that he is head of his church,[1]
the one through whom the Father rules all things.[2]

[1] Eph. 1:20-23; Col. 1:18
[2] Matt. 28:18; John 5:22-23

**51 Q. How does this glory of Christ our head
benefit us?**

A. First, through his Holy Spirit
he pours out gifts from heaven
upon us his members.[1]

Second, by his power
he defends us and keeps us safe
from all enemies.[2]

[1] Acts 2:33; Eph. 4:7-12
[2] Ps. 110:1-2; John 10:27-30; Rev. 19:11-16

**52 Q. How does Christ's return
"to judge the living and the dead"
comfort you?**

A. In all distress and persecution,
with uplifted head,
I confidently await the very judge
who has already offered himself to the judgment of God
in my place and removed the whole curse from me.[1]
Christ will cast all his enemies and mine
into everlasting condemnation,
but will take me and all his chosen ones
to himself
into the joy and glory of heaven.[2]

[1] Luke 21:28; Rom. 8:22-25; Phil. 3:20-21; Tit. 2:13-14
[2] Matt. 25:31-46; 2 Thess. 1:6-10

LORD'S DAY 20

**53 Q. What do you believe
concerning "the Holy Spirit"?**
   A. First, that the Spirit, with the Father and the Son,
     is eternal God.[1]

     Second, that the Spirit is given also to me,[2]
      so that, through true faith,
      he makes me share in Christ and all his benefits,[3]
      comforts me,[4]
      and will remain with me forever.[5]

[1] Gen. 1:1-2; Matt. 28:19; Acts 5:3-4
[2] 1 Cor. 6:19; 2 Cor. 1:21-22; Gal. 4:6
[3] Gal. 3:14
[4] John 15:26; Acts 9:31
[5] John 14:16-17; 1 Pet. 4:14

**54 Q. What do you believe
concerning "the holy catholic church"?**

A. I believe that the Son of God
through his Spirit and Word,[1]
out of the entire human race,[2]
from the beginning of the world to its end,[3]
gathers, protects, and preserves for himself
a community chosen for eternal life[4]
and united in true faith.[5]
And of this community I am[6] and always will be[7]
a living member.

[1] John 10:14-16; Acts 20:28; Rom. 10:14-17; Col. 1:18
[2] Gen. 26:3b-4; Rev. 5:9
[3] Isa. 59:21; 1 Cor. 11:26
[4] Matt. 16:18; John 10:28-30; Rom. 8:28-30; Eph. 1:3-14
[5] Acts 2:42-47; Eph. 4:1-6
[6] 1 John 3:14, 19-21
[7] John 10:27-28; 1 Cor. 1:4-9; 1 Pet. 1:3-5

**55 Q. What do you understand by
"the communion of saints"?**

A. First, that believers one and all,
as members of this community,
share in Christ
and in all his treasures and gifts.[1]

Second, that each member
should consider it a duty
to use these gifts
readily and joyfully
for the service and enrichment
of the other members.[2]

[1] Rom. 8:32; 1 Cor. 6:17; 12:4-7, 12-13; 1 John 1:3
[2] Rom. 12:4-8; 1 Cor. 12:20-27; 13:1-7; Phil. 2:4-8

56 Q. What do you believe
concerning "the forgiveness of sins"?
   A. I believe that God,
         because of Christ's satisfaction,
      will no longer remember
         any of my sins[1]
         or my sinful nature
            which I need to struggle against all my life.[2]

      Rather, by grace
         God grants me the righteousness of Christ
         to free me forever from judgment.[3]

[1] Ps. 103:3-4, 10, 12; Mic. 7:18-19; 2 Cor. 5:18-21; 1 John 1:7; 2:2
[2] Rom. 7:21-25
[3] John 3:17-18; Rom. 8:1-2

57 Q. How does "the resurrection of the body" comfort you?

   A. Not only will my soul
       be taken immediately after this life
       to Christ its head,[1]
    but also my very flesh will be
       raised by the power of Christ,
       reunited with my soul,
       and made like Christ's glorious body.[2]

[1] Luke 23:43; Phil. 1:21-23
[2] 1 Cor. 15:20, 42-46, 54; Phil. 3:21; 1 John 3:2

58 Q. How does the article concerning "life everlasting" comfort you?

   A. Even as I already now
       experience in my heart
       the beginning of eternal joy,[1]
    so after this life I will have
       perfect blessedness such as
          no eye has seen,
          no ear has heard,
          no human heart has ever imagined:
    a blessedness in which to praise God forever.[2]

[1] Rom. 14:17
[2] John 17:3; 1 Cor. 2:9

**59 Q. What good does it do you, however,
      to believe all this?**
    A. In Christ I am righteous before God
       and heir to life everlasting.[1]

[1] John 3:36; Rom. 1:17 (Hab. 2:4); Rom. 5:1-2

60 Q. How are you righteous before God?
    A. Only by true faith in Jesus Christ.[1]

    Even though my conscience accuses me
       of having grievously sinned against all God's
         commandments,
       of never having kept any of them,[2]
       and of still being inclined toward all evil,[3]
    nevertheless,
       without any merit of my own,[4]
       out of sheer grace,[5]
    God grants and credits to me
    the perfect satisfaction, righteousness, and holiness of
       Christ,[6]
       as if I had never sinned nor been a sinner,
       and as if I had been as perfectly obedient
         as Christ was obedient for me.[7]

    All I need to do
    is accept this gift with a believing heart.[8]

[1] Rom. 3:21-28; Gal. 2:16; Eph. 2:8-9; Phil 3:8-11
[2] Rom. 3:9-10
[3] Rom. 7:23
[4] Tit. 3:4-5
[5] Rom. 3:24; Eph. 2:8
[6] Rom. 4:3-5 (Gen. 15:6); 2 Cor. 5:17-19; 1 John 2:1-2
[7] Rom. 4:24-25; 2 Cor. 5:21
[8] John 3:18; Acts 16:30-31

**61 Q. Why do you say that
through faith alone
you are righteous?**

A. Not because I please God
by the worthiness of my faith.
It is because only Christ's satisfaction, righteousness, and
holiness
make me righteous before God,[1]
and because I can accept this righteousness and make it mine
in no other way
than through faith.[2]

[1] 1 Cor. 1:30-31
[2] Rom. 10:10; 1 John 5:10-12

62 Q. **Why can't our good works**
 be our righteousness before God,
 or at least a part of our righteousness?

A. Because the righteousness
 which can pass God's judgment
 must be entirely perfect
 and must in every way measure up to the divine law.[1]
 But even our best works in this life
 are imperfect
 and stained with sin.[2]

[1] Rom. 3:20; Gal. 3:10 (Deut. 27:26)
[2] Isa. 64:6

63 Q. **How can our good works**
 be said to merit nothing
 when God promises to reward them
 in this life and the next?[1]

A. This reward is not earned;
 it is a gift of grace.[2]

[1] Matt. 5:12; Heb. 11:6
[2] Luke 17:10; 2 Tim. 4:7-8

64 Q. **But doesn't this teaching**
 make people indifferent and wicked?

A. No.
 It is impossible
 for those grafted into Christ through true faith
 not to produce fruits of gratitude.[1]

[1] Luke 6:43-45; John 15:5

LORD'S DAY 25

65 Q. **It is through faith alone**
       that we share in Christ and all his benefits:
       where then does that faith come from?
    A. The Holy Spirit produces it in our hearts[1]
          by the preaching of the holy gospel,[2]
       and confirms it
          by the use of the holy sacraments.[3]

[1] John 3:5; 1 Cor. 2:10-14; Eph. 2:8
[2] Rom. 10:17; 1 Pet. 1:23-25
[3] Matt. 28:19-20; 1 Cor. 10:16

66 Q. **What are sacraments?**
    A. Sacraments are visible, holy signs and seals.
       They were instituted by God so that
          by our use of them
       he might make us understand more clearly
          the promise of the gospel,
       and seal that promise.[1]

       And this is God's gospel promise:
          to grant us forgiveness of sins and eternal life
             by grace
             because of Christ's one sacrifice
             accomplished on the cross.[2]

[1] Gen. 17:11; Deut. 30:6; Rom. 4:11
[2] Matt. 26:27-28; Acts 2:38; Heb. 10:10

67 Q. Are both the word and the sacraments then
       intended to focus our faith
       on the sacrifice of Jesus Christ on the cross
       as the only ground of our salvation?
    A. Yes!
       In the gospel the Holy Spirit teaches us
       and by the holy sacraments confirms
          that our entire salvation
          rests on Christ's one sacrifice for us on the cross.[1]

[1] Rom. 6:3; 1 Cor. 11:26; Gal. 3:27

68 Q. How many sacraments
       did Christ institute in the New Testament?
    A. Two: holy baptism and the holy supper.[1]

[1] Matt. 28:19-20; 1 Cor. 11:23-26

LORD'S DAY 26

69 Q. **How does holy baptism**
remind and assure you
that Christ's one sacrifice on the cross
benefits you personally?

A. In this way:
Christ instituted this outward washing[1]
and with it promised that,
    as surely as water washes away the dirt from the body,
    so certainly his blood and his Spirit
    wash away my soul's impurity,
        that is, all my sins.[2]

[1] Acts 2:38
[2] Matt. 3:11; Rom. 6:3-10; 1 Pet. 3:21

70 Q. **What does it mean**
to be washed with Christ's blood and Spirit?

A. To be washed with Christ's blood means
    that God, by grace, has forgiven our sins
      because of Christ's blood
      poured out for us in his sacrifice on the cross.[1]

To be washed with Christ's Spirit means
    that the Holy Spirit has renewed
    and sanctified us to be members of Christ,
      so that more and more
        we become dead to sin
        and live holy and blameless lives.[2]

[1] Zech. 13:1; Eph. 1:7-8; Heb. 12:24; 1 Pet. 1:2; Rev. 1:5
[2] Ezek. 36:25-27; John 3:5-8; Rom. 6:4; 1 Cor. 6:11; Col. 2:11-12

71 **Q.** Where does Christ promise
that we are washed with his blood and Spirit
as surely as we are washed
with the water of baptism?

A. In the institution of baptism, where he says:

"Go therefore and make disciples of all nations,
baptizing them in the name of the Father
and of the Son
and of the Holy Spirit."[1]

"The one who believes and is baptized will be saved;
but the one who does not believe will be condemned."[2]

This promise is repeated when Scripture calls baptism
"the water of rebirth"[3] and
the washing away of sins.[4]

[1] Matt. 28:19
[2] Mark 16:16
[3] Tit. 3:5
[4] Acts 22:16

**72 Q. Does this outward washing with water
itself wash away sins?**

A. No, only Jesus Christ's blood and the Holy Spirit
cleanse us from all sins.[1]

[1] Matt. 3:11; 1 Pet. 3:21; 1 John 1:7

**73 Q. Why then does the Holy Spirit call baptism
the water of rebirth and
the washing away of sins?**

A. God has good reason for these words.
To begin with, God wants to teach us that
the blood and Spirit of Christ take away our sins
just as water removes dirt from the body.[1]

But more important,
God wants to assure us, by this divine pledge and sign,
that we are as truly washed of our sins spiritually
as our bodies are washed with water physically.[2]

[1] 1 Cor. 6:11; Rev. 1:5; 7:14
[2] Acts 2:38; Rom. 6:3-4; Gal. 3:27

74 Q. Should infants also be baptized?

A. Yes.
Infants as well as adults
are included in God's covenant and people,[1]
and they, no less than adults, are promised
deliverance from sin through Christ's blood
and the Holy Spirit who produces faith.[2]

Therefore, by baptism, the sign of the covenant,
they too should be incorporated into the Christian church
and distinguished from the children
of unbelievers.[3]
This was done in the Old Testament by circumcision,[4]
which was replaced in the New Testament by baptism.[5]

[1] Gen. 17:7; Matt. 19:14
[2] Isa. 44:1-3; Acts 2:38-39; 16:31
[3] Acts 10:47; 1 Cor. 7:14
[4] Gen. 17:9-14
[5] Col. 2:11-13

LORD'S DAY 28

75 Q. **How does the holy supper**
        remind and assure you
        that you share in
        Christ's one sacrifice on the cross
        and in all his benefits?

     A. In this way:
         Christ has commanded me and all believers
         to eat this broken bread and to drink this cup
         in remembrance of him.
         With this command come these promises:[1]

         First,
             as surely as I see with my eyes
                 the bread of the Lord broken for me
                 and the cup shared with me,
             so surely
                 his body was offered and broken for me
                 and his blood poured out for me
                     on the cross.

         Second,
             as surely as
                 I receive from the hand of the one who serves,
                 and taste with my mouth
                     the bread and cup of the Lord,
                     given me as sure signs of Christ's body and blood,
             so surely
                 he nourishes and refreshes my soul for eternal life
                 with his crucified body and poured-out blood.

[1] Matt. 26:26-28; Mark 14:22-24; Luke 22:19-20; 1 Cor. 11:23-25

**76 Q. What does it mean
to eat the crucified body of Christ
and to drink his poured-out blood?**

   A. It means
to accept with a believing heart
the entire suffering and death of Christ
and thereby
to receive forgiveness of sins and eternal life.[1]

But it means more.
Through the Holy Spirit, who lives both in Christ and in us,
we are united more and more to Christ's blessed body.[2]
And so, although he is in heaven[3] and we are on earth,
we are flesh of his flesh and bone of his bone.[4]
And we forever live on and are governed by one Spirit,
as the members of our body are by one soul.[5]

[1] John 6:35, 40, 50-54
[2] John 6:55-56; 1 Cor. 12:13
[3] Acts 1:9-11; 1 Cor. 11:26; Col. 3:1
[4] 1 Cor. 6:15-17; Eph. 5:29-30; 1 John 4:13
[5] John 6:56-58; 15:1-6; Eph. 4:15-16; 1 John 3:24

**77 Q. Where does Christ promise
to nourish and refresh believers
with his body and blood
as surely as
they eat this broken bread
and drink this cup?**

A. In the institution of the Lord's Supper:

"The Lord Jesus on the night when he was betrayed
took a loaf of bread, and when he had given thanks,
he broke it and said,
    'This is my body that is [broken]* for you.
    Do this in remembrance of me.'
In the same way he took the cup also, after supper, saying,
    'This cup is the new covenant in my blood.
    Do this, as often as you drink it,
    in remembrance of me.'
For as often as you eat this bread and drink the cup,
you proclaim the Lord's death
until he comes."[1]

This promise is repeated by Paul in these words:

"The cup of blessing that we bless,
    is it not a sharing in the blood of Christ?
The bread that we break,
    is it not a sharing in the body of Christ?
Because there is one bread, we who are many are one body,
for we all partake of the one bread."[2]

[1] 1 Cor. 11:23-26
[2] 1 Cor. 10:16-17
*The word "broken" does not appear in the NRSV text, but it was present in the original German of the Heidelberg Catechism.

**78 Q. Do the bread and wine become
the real body and blood of Christ?**

  A. No.
  Just as the water of baptism
    is not changed into Christ's blood
    and does not itself wash away sins
    but is simply a divine sign and assurance[1] of these things,
  so too the holy bread of the Lord's Supper
    does not become the actual body of Christ,[2]
    even though it is called the body of Christ[3]
      in keeping with the nature and language of sacraments.[4]

[1] Eph. 5:26; Tit. 3:5
[2] Matt. 26:26-29
[3] 1 Cor. 10:16-17; 11:26-28
[4] Gen. 17:10-11; Ex. 12:11, 13; 1 Cor. 10:1-4

**79 Q. Why then does Christ call
the bread his body
and the cup his blood,
or the new covenant in his blood,
and Paul use the words,
a sharing in Christ's body and blood?**

  A. Christ has good reason for these words.
  He wants to teach us that
    just as bread and wine nourish the temporal life,
    so too his crucified body and poured-out blood
    are the true food and drink of our souls for eternal life.[1]

  But more important,
  he wants to assure us, by this visible sign and pledge,
    that we, through the Holy Spirit's work,
      share in his true body and blood
      as surely as our mouths
      receive these holy signs in his remembrance,[2]
    and that all of his suffering and obedience
      are as definitely ours
      as if we personally
        had suffered and made satisfaction for our sins.[3]

[1] John 6:51, 55
[2] 1 Cor. 10:16-17; 11:26
[3] Rom. 6:5-11

**80* Q. How does the Lord's Supper
     differ from the Roman Catholic Mass?**

   A. The Lord's Supper declares to us
          that all our sins are completely forgiven
          through the one sacrifice of Jesus Christ,
          which he himself accomplished on the cross once for all.[1]
       It also declares to us
          that the Holy Spirit grafts us into Christ,[2]
          who with his true body
          is now in heaven at the right hand of the Father[3]
          where he wants us to worship him.[4]

       [But the Mass teaches
          that the living and the dead
          do not have their sins forgiven
          through the suffering of Christ
          unless Christ is still offered for them daily by the priests.
       It also teaches
          that Christ is bodily present
          under the form of bread and wine
          where Christ is therefore to be worshiped.
       Thus the Mass is basically
          nothing but a denial
          of the one sacrifice and suffering of Jesus Christ
          and a condemnable idolatry.]**

[1] John 19:30; Heb. 7:27; 9:12, 25-26; 10:10-18
[2] 1 Cor. 6:17; 10:16-17
[3] Acts 7:55-56; Heb. 1:3; 8:1
[4] Matt. 6:20-21; John 4:21-24; Phil. 3:20; Col. 3:1-3

*Q&A 80 was altogether absent from the first edition of the catechism but was present in a shorter form in the second edition. The translation here given is of the expanded text of the third edition.

**In response to a mandate from Synod 1998, the Christian Reformed Church's Interchurch Relations Committee conducted a study of Q&A 80 and the Roman Catholic Mass. Based on this study, Synod 2004 declared that "Q&A 80 can no longer be held in its current form as part of our confession." Synod 2006 directed that Q&A 80 remain in the CRC's text of the Heidelberg Catechism but that the last three paragraphs be placed in brackets to indicate that they do not accurately reflect the official teaching and practice of today's Roman Catholic Church and are no longer confessionally binding on members of the CRC.

The Reformed Church in America retains the original full text, choosing to recognize that the catechism was written within a historical context which may not accurately describe the Roman Catholic Church's current stance.

81 Q. **Who should come**
       to the Lord's table?

    A. Those who are displeased with themselves
          because of their sins,
       but who nevertheless trust
          that their sins are pardoned
          and that their remaining weakness is covered
             by the suffering and death of Christ,
       and who also desire more and more
          to strengthen their faith
          and to lead a better life.

    Hypocrites and those who are unrepentant, however,
    eat and drink judgment on themselves.[1]

[1] 1 Cor. 10:19-22; 11:26-32

82 Q. **Should those be admitted**
       to the Lord's Supper
       who show by what they profess and how they live
       that they are unbelieving and ungodly?

    A. No, that would dishonor God's covenant
       and bring down God's wrath upon the entire congregation.[1]
       Therefore, according to the instruction of Christ
          and his apostles,
          the Christian church is duty-bound to exclude such people,
             by the official use of the keys of the kingdom,
          until they reform their lives.

[1] 1 Cor. 11:17-32; Ps. 50:14-16; Isa. 1:11-17

83 Q. What are the keys of the kingdom?
    A. The preaching of the holy gospel
      and Christian discipline toward repentance.
      Both of them
          open the kingdom of heaven to believers
          and close it to unbelievers.[1]

[1] Matt. 16:19; John 20:22-23

84 Q. How does preaching the holy gospel
      open and close the kingdom of heaven?
    A. According to the command of Christ:

      The kingdom of heaven is opened
      by proclaiming and publicly declaring
          to all believers, each and every one, that,
          as often as they accept the gospel promise in true faith,
          God, because of Christ's merit,
          truly forgives all their sins.

      The kingdom of heaven is closed, however,
      by proclaiming and publicly declaring
          to unbelievers and hypocrites that,
          as long as they do not repent,
          the wrath of God and eternal condemnation
          rest on them.

      God's judgment, both in this life and in the life to come,
      is based on this gospel testimony.[1]

[1] Matt. 16:19; John 3:31-36; 20:21-23

**85 Q. How is the kingdom of heaven
closed and opened by Christian discipline?**

A. According to the command of Christ:

Those who, though called Christians,
    profess unchristian teachings or live unchristian lives,
and who after repeated personal and loving admonitions,
    refuse to abandon their errors and evil ways,
and who after being reported to the church, that is,
        to those ordained by the church for that purpose,
    fail to respond also to the church's admonitions—
such persons the church excludes
        from the Christian community
    by withholding the sacraments from them,
and God also excludes them from the kingdom of Christ.[1]

Such persons,
    when promising and demonstrating genuine reform,
are received again
    as members of Christ
    and of his church.[2]

[1] Matt. 18:15-20; 1 Cor. 5:3-5, 11-13; 2 Thess. 3:14-15
[2] Luke 15:20-24; 2 Cor. 2:6-11

Part III: Gratitude

LORD'S DAY 32

86 Q. **Since we have been delivered**
from our misery
by grace through Christ
without any merit of our own,
why then should we do good works?
   A. Because Christ, having redeemed us by his blood,
      is also restoring us by his Spirit into his image,
         so that with our whole lives
            we may show that we are thankful to God
               for his benefits,[1]
         so that he may be praised through us,[2]
         so that we may be assured of our faith by its fruits,[3]
         and so that by our godly living
            our neighbors may be won over to Christ.[4]

[1] Rom. 6:13; 12:1-2; 1 Pet. 2:5-10
[2] Matt. 5:16; 1 Cor. 6:19-20
[3] Matt. 7:17-18; Gal. 5:22-24; 2 Pet. 1:10-11
[4] Matt. 5:14-16; Rom. 14:17-19; 1 Pet. 2:12; 3:1-2

87 Q. **Can those be saved**
who do not turn to God
from their ungrateful
and unrepentant ways?
   A. By no means.
      Scripture tells us that
         no unchaste person,
         no idolater, adulterer, thief,
         no covetous person,
         no drunkard, slanderer, robber,
         or the like
         will inherit the kingdom of God.[1]

[1] 1 Cor. 6:9-10; Gal. 5:19-21; Eph. 5:1-20; 1 John 3:14

**88 Q. What is involved
in genuine repentance or conversion?**
  A. Two things:
    the dying-away of the old self,
    and the rising-to-life of the new.[1]

[1] Rom. 6:1-11; 2 Cor. 5:17; Eph. 4:22-24; Col. 3:5-10

89 Q. What is the dying-away of the old self?
  A. To be genuinely sorry for sin
    and more and more to hate
    and run away from it.[1]

[1] Ps. 51:3-4, 17; Joel 2:12-13; Rom. 8:12-13; 2 Cor. 7:10

90 Q. What is the rising-to-life of the new self?
  A. Wholehearted joy in God through Christ[1]
    and a love and delight to live
      according to the will of God
      by doing every kind of good work.[2]

[1] Ps. 51:8, 12; Isa.57:15; Rom. 5:1; 14:17
[2] Rom. 6:10-11; Gal. 2:20

91 Q. What are good works?
  A. Only those which
      are done out of true faith,[1]
      conform to God's law,[2]
      and are done for God's glory;[3]
    and not those based
      on our own opinion
      or human tradition.[4]

[1] John 15:5; Heb. 11:6
[2] Lev. 18:4; 1 Sam. 15:22; Eph. 2:10
[3] 1 Cor. 10:31
[4] Deut. 12:32; Isa. 29:13; Ezek. 20:18-19; Matt. 15:7-9

LORD'S DAY 34

92 Q. What is God's law?
    A. God spoke all these words:

THE FIRST COMMANDMENT
    "I am the LORD your God,
        who brought you out of the land of Egypt,
        out of the house of slavery;
    you shall have no other gods before me."

THE SECOND COMMANDMENT
    "You shall not make for yourself an idol,
        whether in the form of anything that is in heaven above,
        or that is on the earth beneath,
        or that is in the water under the earth.
    You shall not bow down to them or worship them;
        for I the LORD your God am a jealous God,
        punishing children for the iniquity of parents,
            to the third and the fourth generation
            of those who reject me,
        but showing love to the thousandth generation of those
            who love me and keep my commandments."

THE THIRD COMMANDMENT
    "You shall not make wrongful use of the name of the LORD
        your God,
        for the LORD will not acquit anyone
        who misuses his name."

THE FOURTH COMMANDMENT

"Remember the sabbath day, and keep it holy.
Six days you shall labor and do all your work.
But the seventh day is a sabbath to the LORD your God;
you shall not do any work—
  you, your son or your daughter,
  your male or female slave,
  your livestock,
  or the alien resident in your towns.
For in six days the LORD made
  heaven and earth, the sea,
  and all that is in them,
but rested the seventh day;
therefore the LORD blessed the sabbath day
and consecrated it."

THE FIFTH COMMANDMENT

"Honor your father and your mother,
  so that your days may be long
  in the land that the LORD your God is giving to you."

THE SIXTH COMMANDMENT

"You shall not murder."

THE SEVENTH COMMANDMENT

"You shall not commit adultery."

THE EIGHTH COMMANDMENT

"You shall not steal."

THE NINTH COMMANDMENT

"You shall not bear false witness
  against your neighbor."

THE TENTH COMMANDMENT

"You shall not covet your neighbor's house;
you shall not covet your neighbor's wife,
  or male or female slave,
  or ox, or donkey,
  or anything that belongs to your neighbor."[1]

[1] Ex. 20:1-17; Deut. 5:6-21

93 Q. How are these commandments divided?

    A. Into two tables.
        The first has four commandments,
           teaching us how we ought to live in relation to God.
        The second has six commandments,
           teaching us what we owe our neighbor.[1]

[1] Matt. 22:37-39

94 Q. What does the Lord require
        in the first commandment?

    A. That I, not wanting to endanger my own salvation,
        avoid and shun
           all idolatry,[1] sorcery, superstitious rites,[2]
           and prayer to saints or to other creatures.[3]

        That I rightly know the only true God,[4]
           trust him alone,[5]
           and look to God for every good thing[6]
               humbly[7] and patiently,[8]
           and love,[9] fear,[10] and honor[11] God
               with all my heart.
        In short,
           that I give up anything
           rather than go against God's will in any way.[12]

[1] 1 Cor. 6:9-10; 10:5-14; 1 John 5:21
[2] Lev. 19:31; Deut. 18:9-12
[3] Matt. 4:10; Rev. 19:10; 22:8-9
[4] John 17:3
[5] Jer. 17:5, 7
[6] Ps. 104:27-28; James 1:17
[7] 1 Pet. 5:5-6
[8] Col. 1:11; Heb. 10:36
[9] Matt. 22:37 (Deut. 6:5)
[10] Prov. 9:10; 1 Pet. 1:17
[11] Matt. 4:10 (Deut. 6:13)
[12] Matt. 5:29-30; 10:37-39

95 Q. What is idolatry?

    A. Idolatry is
        having or inventing something in which one trusts
        in place of or alongside of the only true God,
           who has revealed himself in the Word.[1]

[1] 1 Chron. 16:26; Gal. 4:8-9; Eph. 5:5; Phil. 3:19

**96 Q. What is God's will for us
in the second commandment?**
   A. That we in no way make any image of God[1]
   nor worship him in any other way
   than has been commanded in God's Word.[2]

[1] Deut. 4:15-19; Isa. 40:18-25; Acts 17:29; Rom. 1:22-23
[2] Lev. 10:1-7; 1 Sam. 15:22-23; John 4:23-24

**97 Q. May we then not make
any image at all?**
   A. God can not and may not
   be visibly portrayed in any way.

   Although creatures may be portrayed,
   yet God forbids making or having such images
   if one's intention is to worship them
   or to serve God through them.[1]

[1] Ex. 34:13-14, 17; 2 Kings 18:4-5

**98 Q. But may not images be permitted in churches
in place of books for the unlearned?**
   A. No, we should not try to be wiser than God.
   God wants the Christian community instructed
   by the living preaching of his Word—[1]
   not by idols that cannot even talk.[2]

[1] Rom. 10:14-15, 17; 2 Tim. 3:16-17; 2 Pet. 1:19
[2] Jer. 10:8; Hab. 2:18-20

99 Q. What is the aim of the third commandment?

   A. That we neither blaspheme nor misuse the name of God
         by cursing,[1] perjury,[2] or unnecessary oaths,[3]
      nor share in such horrible sins
         by being silent bystanders.[4]

      In summary,
         we should use the holy name of God
            only with reverence and awe,[5]
         so that we may properly
            confess God,[6]
            pray to God,[7]
            and glorify God in all our words and works.[8]

[1] Lev. 24:10-17
[2] Lev. 19:12
[3] Matt. 5:37; James 5:12
[4] Lev. 5:1; Prov. 29:24
[5] Ps. 99:1-5; Jer. 4:2
[6] Matt. 10:32-33; Rom. 10:9-10
[7] Ps. 50:14-15; 1 Tim. 2:8
[8] Col. 3:17

**100 Q. Is blasphemy of God's name by swearing and cursing
         really such serious sin
         that God is angry also with those
         who do not do all they can
         to help prevent and forbid it?**

   A. Yes, indeed.[1]
         No sin is greater
         or provokes God's wrath more
         than blaspheming his name.
      That is why God commanded it to be punished with death.[2]

[1] Lev. 5:1
[2] Lev. 24:10-17

**101 Q. But may we swear an oath in God's name
     if we do it reverently?**

    A. Yes, when the government demands it,
        or when necessity requires it,
            in order to maintain and promote truth and
                trustworthiness
            for God's glory and our neighbor's good.

        Such oaths are grounded in God's Word[1]
            and were rightly used by the people of God
                in the Old and New Testaments.[2]

[1] Deut. 6:13; 10:20; Jer. 4:1-2; Heb. 6:16
[2] Gen. 21:24; Josh. 9:15; 1 Kings 1:29-30; Rom. 1:9; 2 Cor. 1:23

102 Q. May we also swear by saints or other creatures?

    A. No.
        A legitimate oath means calling upon God
        as the only one who knows my heart
            to witness to my truthfulness
            and to punish me if I swear falsely.[1]
        No creature is worthy of such honor.[2]

[1] Rom. 9:1; 2 Cor. 1:23
[2] Matt. 5:34-37; 23:16-22; James 5:12

**103 Q. What is God's will for you
in the fourth commandment?**

   A. First,

        that the gospel ministry and education for it be
           maintained,[1]
        and that, especially on the festive day of rest,
        I diligently attend the assembly of God's people[2]
           to learn what God's Word teaches,[3]
           to participate in the sacraments,[4]
           to pray to God publicly,[5]
           and to bring Christian offerings for the poor.[6]

      Second,

        that every day of my life
           I rest from my evil ways,
           let the Lord work in me through his Spirit,
        and so begin in this life
        the eternal Sabbath.[7]

[1] Deut. 6:4-9, 20-25; 1 Cor. 9:13-14; 2 Tim. 2:2; 3:13-17; Tit. 1:5
[2] Deut. 12:5-12; Ps. 40:9-10; 68:26; Acts 2:42-47; Heb. 10:23-25
[3] Rom. 10:14-17; 1 Cor. 14:31-32; 1 Tim. 4:13
[4] 1 Cor. 11:23-25
[5] Col. 3:16; 1 Tim. 2:1
[6] Ps. 50:14; 1 Cor. 16:2; 2 Cor. 8 & 9
[7] Isa. 66:23; Heb. 4:9-11

**104 Q. What is God's will for you
in the fifth commandment?**

   A. That I honor, love, and be loyal
         to my father and mother
         and all those in authority over me;
      that I submit myself with proper obedience
         to all their good teaching and discipline;[1]
      and also that I be patient with their failings—[2]
      for through them God chooses to rule us.[3]

[1] Ex. 21:17; Prov. 1:8; 4:1; Rom. 13:1-2; Eph. 5:21-22; 6:1-9; Col. 3:18- 4:1
[2] Prov. 20:20; 23:22; 1 Pet. 2:18
[3] Matt. 22:21; Rom. 13:1-8; Eph. 6:1-9; Col. 3:18-21

**105 Q. What is God's will for you
in the sixth commandment?**
A. I am not to belittle, hate, insult, or kill my neighbor—
not by my thoughts, my words, my look or gesture,
and certainly not by actual deeds—
and I am not to be party to this in others;[1]
rather, I am to put away all desire for revenge.[2]

I am not to harm or recklessly endanger myself either.[3]
Prevention of murder is also why
government is armed with the sword.[4]

[1] Gen. 9:6; Lev. 19:17-18; Matt. 5:21-22; 26:52
[2] Prov. 25:21-22; Matt. 18:35; Rom. 12:19; Eph. 4:26
[3] Matt. 4:7; 26:52; Rom. 13:11-14
[4] Gen. 9:6; Ex. 21:14; Rom. 13:4

106 Q. Does this commandment refer only to murder?
A. By forbidding murder God teaches us
that he hates the root of murder:
envy, hatred, anger, vindictiveness.[1]

In God's sight all such are disguised forms of murder.[2]

[1] Prov. 14:30; Rom. 1:29; 12:19; Gal. 5:19-21; 1 John 2:9-11
[2] 1 John 3:15

**107 Q. Is it enough then
that we do not murder our neighbor
in any such way?**
A. No.
By condemning envy, hatred, and anger
God wants us
to love our neighbors as ourselves,[1]
to be patient, peace-loving, gentle,
merciful, and friendly toward them,[2]
to protect them from harm as much as we can,
and to do good even to our enemies.[3]

[1] Matt. 7:12; 22:39; Rom. 12:10
[2] Matt. 5:3-12; Luke 6:36; Rom. 12:10, 18; Gal. 6:1-2; Eph. 4:2; Col. 3:12; 1 Pet. 3:8
[3] Ex. 23:4-5; Matt. 5:44-45; Rom. 12:20-21 (Prov. 25:21-22)

108 Q. What does the seventh commandment teach us?

   A. That God condemns all unchastity,[1]
      and that therefore we should thoroughly detest it[2]
      and live decent and chaste lives,[3]
      within or outside of the holy state of marriage.

[1] Lev. 18:30; Eph. 5:3-5
[2] Jude 22-23
[3] 1 Cor. 7:1-9; 1 Thess. 4:3-8; Heb. 13:4

**109 Q. Does God, in this commandment,
      forbid only such scandalous sins as adultery?**

   A. We are temples of the Holy Spirit, body and soul,
      and God wants both to be kept clean and holy.
      That is why God forbids
         all unchaste actions, looks, talk, thoughts, or desires,[1]
         and whatever may incite someone to them.[2]

[1] Matt. 5:27-29; 1 Cor. 6:18-20; Eph. 5:3-4
[2] 1 Cor. 15:33; Eph. 5:18

**110 Q. What does God forbid
in the eighth commandment?**

    A. God forbids not only outright theft and robbery,
        punishable by law.[1]

        But in God's sight theft also includes
        all scheming and swindling
        in order to get our neighbor's goods for ourselves,
            whether by force or means that appear legitimate,[2]
            such as
                inaccurate measurements of weight, size, or volume;
                fraudulent merchandising;
                counterfeit money;
                excessive interest;
                or any other means forbidden by God.[3]

        In addition God forbids all greed[4]
        and pointless squandering of his gifts.[5]

[1] Ex. 22:1; 1 Cor. 5:9-10; 6:9-10
[2] Mic. 6:9-11; Luke 3:14; James 5:1-6
[3] Deut. 25:13-16; Ps. 15:5; Prov. 11:1; 12:22; Ezek. 45:9-12; Luke 6:35
[4] Luke 12:15; Eph. 5:5
[5] Prov. 21:20; 23:20-21; Luke 16:10-13

**111 Q. What does God require of you
in this commandment?**

    A. That I do whatever I can
            for my neighbor's good,
        that I treat others
            as I would like them to treat me,
        and that I work faithfully
            so that I may share with those in need.[1]

[1] Isa. 58:5-10; Matt. 7:12; Gal. 6:9-10; Eph. 4:28

112 Q. What is the aim of the ninth commandment?
   A. That I
           never give false testimony against anyone,
           twist no one's words,
           not gossip or slander,
           nor join in condemning anyone
           rashly or without a hearing.[1]

   Rather, in court and everywhere else,
   I should avoid lying and deceit of every kind;
       these are the very devices the devil uses,
       and they would call down on me God's intense wrath.[2]
   I should love the truth,
       speak it candidly,
       and openly acknowledge it.[3]
   And I should do what I can
       to guard and advance my neighbor's good name.[4]

[1] Ps. 15; Prov. 19:5; Matt. 7:1; Luke 6:37; Rom. 1:28-32
[2] Lev. 19:11-12; Prov. 12:22; 13:5; John 8:44; Rev. 21:8
[3] 1 Cor. 13:6; Eph. 4:25
[4] 1 Pet. 3:8-9; 4:8

113 Q. What is the aim of the tenth commandment?

    A. That not even the slightest desire or thought
contrary to any one of God's commandments
should ever arise in our hearts.

    Rather, with all our hearts
we should always hate sin
and take pleasure in whatever is right.[1]

[1] Ps. 19:7-14; 139:23-24; Rom. 7:7-8

**114 Q. But can those converted to God
obey these commandments perfectly?**

    A. No.
In this life even the holiest
have only a small beginning of this obedience.[1]

    Nevertheless, with all seriousness of purpose,
they do begin to live
according to all, not only some,
of God's commandments.[2]

[1] Eccles. 7:20; Rom. 7:14-15; 1 Cor. 13:9; 1 John 1:8-10
[2] Ps. 1:1-2; Rom. 7:22-25; Phil. 3:12-16

115 Q. **Since no one in this life**
       can obey the Ten Commandments perfectly,
       why does God want them
       preached so pointedly?

   A. First, so that the longer we live
          the more we may come to know our sinfulness
          and the more eagerly look to Christ
              for forgiveness of sins and righteousness.[1]

      Second, so that
      we may never stop striving,
      and never stop praying to God for the grace of the Holy
              Spirit,
          to be renewed more and more after God's image,
      until after this life we reach our goal:
          perfection.[2]

[1] Ps. 32:5; Rom. 3:19-26; 7:7, 24-25; 1 John 1:9
[2] 1 Cor. 9:24; Phil. 3:12-14; 1 John 3:1-3

LORD'S DAY 45

116 Q. Why do Christians need to pray?
    A. Because prayer is the most important part
        of the thankfulness God requires of us.[1]
      And also because God gives his grace and Holy Spirit
      only to those who pray continually and groan inwardly,
        asking God for these gifts
        and thanking God for them.[2]

[1] Ps. 50:14-15; 116:12-19; 1 Thess. 5:16-18
[2] Matt. 7:7-8; Luke 11:9-13

117 Q. What is the kind of prayer
      that pleases God and that he listens to?
    A. First, we must pray from the heart
        to no other than the one true God,
            revealed to us in his Word,
        asking for everything God has commanded us to ask for.[1]

      Second, we must fully recognize our need and misery,
        so that we humble ourselves in God's majestic presence.[2]

      Third, we must rest on this unshakable foundation:
        even though we do not deserve it,
        God will surely listen to our prayer
            because of Christ our Lord.
        That is what God promised us in his Word.[3]

[1] Ps. 145:18-20; John 4:22-24; Rom. 8:26-27; James 1:5; 1 John 5:14-15
[2] 2 Chron. 7:14; Ps. 2:11; 34:18; 62:8; Isa. 66:2; Rev. 4
[3] Dan. 9:17-19; Matt. 7:8; John 14:13-14; 16:23; Rom. 10:13; James 1:6

118 Q. What did God command us to pray for?

    A. Everything we need, spiritually and physically,[1]
       as embraced in the prayer
       Christ our Lord himself taught us.

[1] James 1:17; Matt. 6:33

119 Q. What is this prayer?

    A. Our Father in heaven,
       hallowed be your name.
       Your kingdom come.
       Your will be done,
          on earth as it is in heaven.
       Give us this day our daily bread.
       And forgive us our debts,
          as we also have forgiven our debtors.
       And do not bring us to the time of trial,
          but rescue us from the evil one.*
       For the kingdom
          and the power
          and the glory are yours forever.
       Amen.[1]**

[1] Matt. 6:9-13; Luke 11:2-4

*This text of the Lord's Prayer is from the New Revised Standard Version in keeping with the use of the NRSV throughout this edition of the catechism. Most biblical scholars agree that it is an accurate translation of the Greek text and carries virtually the same meaning as the more traditional text of the Lord's Prayer.

**Earlier and better manuscripts of Matthew 6 omit the words "For the kingdom and . . . Amen."

**120 Q. Why did Christ command us
to call God "our Father"?**

   A. To awaken in us
at the very beginning of our prayer
what should be basic to our prayer—
     a childlike reverence and trust
     that through Christ God has become our Father,
and that just as our parents do not refuse us
     the things of this life,
even less will God our Father refuse to give us
     what we ask in faith.[1]

[1] Matt. 7:9-11; Luke 11:11-13

**121 Q. Why the words
"in heaven"?**

   A. These words teach us
     not to think of God's heavenly majesty
      as something earthly,[1]
     and to expect everything
      needed for body and soul
      from God's almighty power.[2]

[1] Jer. 23:23-24; Acts 17:24-25
[2] Matt. 6:25-34; Rom. 8:31-32

122 Q. What does the first petition mean?
    A. "Hallowed be your name" means:

> Help us to truly know you,[1]
> to honor, glorify, and praise you
>   for all your works
>   and for all that shines forth from them:
>   your almighty power, wisdom, kindness,
>   justice, mercy, and truth.[2]

> And it means,

> Help us to direct all our living—
>   what we think, say, and do—
> so that your name will never be blasphemed because of us
> but always honored and praised.[3]

[1] Jer. 9:23-24; 31:33-34; Matt. 16:17; John 17:3
[2] Ex. 34:5-8; Ps. 145; Jer. 32:16-20; Luke 1:46-55, 68-75; Rom. 11:33-36
[3] Ps. 115:1; Matt. 5:16

123 Q. What does the second petition mean?
    A. "Your kingdom come" means:
        Rule us by your Word and Spirit in such a way
            that more and more we submit to you.[1]

        Preserve your church and make it grow.[2]

        Destroy the devil's work;
        destroy every force which revolts against you
        and every conspiracy against your holy Word.[3]
        Do this until your kingdom fully comes,
            when you will be
                all in all.[4]

[1] Ps. 119:5, 105; 143:10; Matt. 6:33
[2] Ps. 122:6-9; Matt. 16:18; Acts 2:42-47
[3] Rom. 16:20; 1 John 3:8
[4] Rom. 8:22-23; 1 Cor. 15:28; Rev. 22:17, 20

124 Q. What does the third petition mean?

    A. "Your will be done, on earth as it is in heaven" means:

      Help us and all people
        to reject our own wills
        and to obey your will without any back talk.
        Your will alone is good.[1]

      Help us one and all to carry out the work we are called to,[2]
        as willingly and faithfully as the angels in heaven.[3]

[1] Matt. 7:21; 16:24-26; Luke 22:42; Rom. 12:1-2; Tit. 2:11-12
[2] 1 Cor. 7:17-24; Eph. 6:5-9
[3] Ps. 103:20-21

125 Q. What does the fourth petition mean?

    A. "Give us this day our daily bread" means:

        Do take care of all our physical needs[1]
        so that we come to know
            that you are the only source of everything good,[2]
            and that neither our work and worry
            nor your gifts
            can do us any good without your blessing.[3]

        And so help us to give up our trust in creatures
        and trust in you alone.[4]

[1] Ps. 104:27-30; 145:15-16; Matt. 6:25-34
[2] Acts 14:17; 17:25; James 1:17
[3] Deut. 8:3; Ps. 37:16; 127:1-2; 1 Cor. 15:58
[4] Ps. 55:22; 62; 146; Jer. 17:5-8; Heb. 13:5-6

126 Q. What does the fifth petition mean?

A. "Forgive us our debts,
as we also have forgiven our debtors" means:

Because of Christ's blood,
do not hold against us, poor sinners that we are,
any of the sins we do
or the evil that constantly clings to us.[1]

Forgive us just as we are fully determined,
as evidence of your grace in us,
to forgive our neighbors.[2]

[1] Ps. 51:1-7; 143:2; Rom. 8:1; 1 John 2:1-2
[2] Matt. 6:14-15; 18:21-35

127 Q. What does the sixth petition mean?
    A. "And do not bring us to the time of trial,
        but rescue us from the evil one" means:

        By ourselves we are too weak
        to hold our own even for a moment.[1]
        And our sworn enemies—
            the devil,[2] the world,[3] and our own flesh—[4]
        never stop attacking us.

        And so, Lord,
        uphold us and make us strong
            with the strength of your Holy Spirit,
        so that we may not go down to defeat
            in this spiritual struggle,[5]
        but may firmly resist our enemies
            until we finally win the complete victory.[6]

[1] Ps. 103:14-16; John 15:1-5
[2] 2 Cor. 11:14; Eph. 6:10-13; 1 Pet. 5:8
[3] John 15:18-21
[4] Rom. 7:23; Gal. 5:17
[5] Matt. 10:19-20; 26:41; Mark 13:33; Rom. 5:3-5
[6] 1 Cor. 10:13; 1 Thess. 3:13; 5:23

128 Q. What does your conclusion to this prayer mean?
    A. "For the kingdom
        and the power
        and the glory are yours forever" means:

        We have made all these petitions of you
        because, as our all-powerful king,
            you are both willing and able
            to give us all that is good;[1]
        and because your holy name,
            and not we ourselves,
        should receive all the praise, forever.[2]

[1] Rom. 10:11-13; 2 Pet. 2:9
[2] Ps. 115:1; John 14:13

129 Q. What does that little word "Amen" express?

  A. "Amen" means:

  This shall truly and surely be!

  It is even more sure
    that God listens to my prayer
  than that I really desire
    what I pray for.[1]

---

[1] Isa. 65:24; 2 Cor. 1:20; 2 Tim. 2:13